CONTENTS

INTRODUCTION ▶️

This book is intended for all *bodhrán* (pronounced "bow-ron") enthusiasts. Whether you're looking to learn the very basics of how to hold and hit the drum, pick up some fundamental patterns, speed drills, and tonal exercises, or learn several advanced tune types to add to your repertoire, this method covers it all while also providing a simple understanding of Irish/Gaelic/Celtic music (often referenced as *trad*) and the bodhrán's role within it. It is important to note that trad is primarily taught by ear. Known as an aural tradition, the music has been passed on from generation to generation by listening rather than writing down. Therefore, it is not necessary to be able to read music to learn the bodhrán or to benefit from this book. There are video clips that go along with each written segment of the book as well as additional diagrams that will guide the player along in the notated portions. The player is highly encouraged to watch the videos. Keep in mind that these instructions only serve as guidelines. Slight adjustments might need to be made along the way to fit what is most comfortable for the player. In holding true to the aural tradition, once the basic techniques are mastered and the player begins to dig deeper into the music, then the focus becomes more about what the player hears and the development of their improvised interpretations rather than strict patterns or written notations.

photo credit: Rick Hokans

ABOUT THE AUTHOR

Amy Richter, a two-time Midwest Fleadh Cheoil champion on the bodhrán, has been performing Irish music since 2003 and teaching since 2007. Most notably, Amy has toured the United States for several years with the world-renowned trad supergroup, Danú. She accompanied them on their televised performance at the 2019 Temple Bar TradFest in Dublin and can be heard on two of their albums, *Ten Thousand Miles* and *An Emerald Isle Christmas*. She's also graced the stage with Lúnasa, Natalie Haas and Alasdair Fraser, John Whelan, John Williams, Liz Carroll and toured the country with Kerry Irish Productions' performance of "An Irish Christmas." Amy is a founding member of áthas (Irish for "joy and happiness"), a Milwaukee, Wisconsin-based band proud to be entertaining their fans since 2005. After studying abroad at the University of Limerick, Amy went on to earn her degree at the University of Wisconsin-Milwaukee. A highly sought-after instructor, Amy has taught both in the United States and Ireland. Locally, she has been a longtime faculty member for the Milwaukee Irish Fest School of Music. Abroad, she's taught alongside some of the greats both at Junior Davey's Bodhrán Academy in County Sligo and virtually at the Búla Buzz international bodhrán summer school. Within the U.S., she's taken the helm for the rhythm workshops at Alasdair Fraser's highly acclaimed Scottish Fiddling School in the Redwoods of California, Valley of the Moon. To follow Amy on her travels, inquire about further instruction, or see if she's playing in a city near you, please visit *www.amyrichter.com*.

HAL LEONARD

BODHRÁN METHOD

BY AMY RICHTER

Video Recorded at DV Productions

Performers: Amy Richter and Heather Lewin

Photographer: Scott Richter

To access video visit:
www.halleonard.com/mylibrary

Enter Code
3346-0188-3823-3920

ISBN 978-1-5400-4431-0

Visit Hal Leonard Online at
www.halleonard.com

Contact us:
Hal Leonard
7777 West Bluemound Road
Milwaukee, WI 53213
Email: info@halleonard.com

In Europe, contact:
Hal Leonard Europe Limited
42 Wigmore Street
Marylebone, London, W1U 2RN
Email: info@halleonardeurope.com

In Australia, contact:
Hal Leonard Australia Pty. Ltd.
4 Lentara Court
Cheltenham, Victoria, 3192 Australia
Email: info@halleonard.com.au

ACKNOWLEDGMENTS

I would like to extend my most sincere and deepest gratitude to the following: my parents, Rick and Julie Richter, who are my ultimate supporters and number one fans. They have been cheering me on since day one (literally!) and have done everything in their power to provide everything and anything to see their daughter "make it" in this world. Thank you to my áthas bandmates, Jeff Ksiazek and Heather Lewin, who have been with me from day one of my musical journey. They continue to be my trad bedrock, always helping me grow as both a player and a person. Many thanks to my big brother and partner in crime growing up, Scotty, for always looking out for his little sister and for taking such great photos for this book! To my sister Kelly, my role model in life: Thank you for always paving the way for your sister. Sincere gratitude to my instructors over the years: David Burns, Mick Dunphy, Patrick Roe, Jackie Moran, Junior Davey, and Paul Phillips, who have not only taught me how to play but have helped in the development of my unique style and opened the door for several performance and teaching opportunities. Endless appreciation to my students, who provide me with countless opportunities in continuing to learn and grow by constantly motivating me to sit down and really analyze what I do and how I do it, therefore equipping me with the skills and comfort level to be able to take on a feat as massive as this tutorial!

Thanks to Kevin Crawford and the members of Danú for allowing me to reach a chapter in my music career that I'd only ever dreamed of. I couldn't have asked for a kinder, more genuine bunch to experience "tour life" with. Many thanks to Hal Leonard for this amazing opportunity. To my colleagues at my day job: Thank you for allowing me to pursue my passion while still paying the bills! And last, but certainly not least: my amazing husband, Logan Penington. Being taught in true trad fashion, I cannot read music. Logan, who also happens to be a drummer (Mannheim Steamroller), helped develop and kindly transcribed all the notated examples in this book (with a tip of the top hat to Chuck Penington!) His patience, love, and positivity have helped me through every step of the way, not only with this book, but in life. It was a fun project for a "couple" of drummers to collaborate on.

To all my family and friends: A simple "thank you" has never felt sufficient enough, but I thoroughly enjoy attempting to extend that gratitude day in and day out. I'm absolutely certain that I would not be where I am today without your endless love and support.

The bodhrán and all the experiences that have come along with it (so far!) have brought me such immense joy and happiness. It has completely transformed my life in the most incredible ways, and my hope is that it brings a bit of *áthas* to you as well!

HISTORY

The bodhrán is a hand-held frame drum. The name comes from the Irish word *bodhar*, meaning "deaf." Found in paintings that date back to the 1800s, the bodhrán is believed to have been around for centuries with its purpose changing over the course of time. Though early examples of bodhrán playing can be heard on 78 rpm discs from the 1920s and 1930s (often labeled as a tambourine), it didn't truly jump into the limelight of Irish music until the 1960s, thanks to Seán Ó Riada. Ó Riada created a band, Ceoltóirí Chualann, which put the bodhrán on the map in a more modern performance context. He brought the instrument much closer to the forefront than ever before and created a launching pad for drummers such as Peadar Mercier and Kevin Conneff (The Chieftains), Johnny "Ringo" McDonagh and Colm Murphy (DeDannan), and Tommy Hayes (Stockton's Wing), who continued to popularize the bodhrán and explore ways to make it sing throughout the '60s and '70s. During the '80s and '90s, players such as Donnchadh Gough (Danú) and Cathy Jordan (Dervish) kept the tradition going strong with their driving rhythms. Marching into the 2000s, John Joe Kelly (Flook), Eamon Murray (Beoga), and Colm Phelan (Goitse) took the drum to even further levels by creating incredibly intricate solos and developing patterns one would usually associate with a drum kit.

Fast forward to today, and it is rare to see an Irish band that does not include a bodhrán. Its popularity has skyrocketed so much so that schools and camps dedicated strictly to the instrument have been created by passionate players and instructors such as Junior Davey (Junior Davey Bodhrán Academy) and Robbie Walsh (Bodhrán Buzz/BúlaBuzz), who strive to pass on their knowledge and excitement of the bodhrán. With loads of players constantly pushing the boundaries, the drum continues to evolve. Makers come up with new ideas, players develop new styles, and teachers continue to educate, therefore securing the tradition and the life of the frame drum for many years to come.

ANATOMY OF THE BODHRÁN ▶️

The drum shell is made of wood, typically ranging from 14"–18" in diameter and 3"–7" in depth. The head is traditionally made of goatskin; however, synthetic heads or other animal skins have been used. The skin is tacked to one side of the drum while the other side is open, allowing the players hand to be placed inside the drum to control the pitch. There may be crossbars inside, but this is increasingly rare on modern drums. The crossbars were originally used to prevent the rim from warping, but modern methods have eliminated the structural purpose of the crossbars. Many drum makers now omit them entirely (or only construct one bar instead of two), so the player is free to move their backhand about the skin. Most modern drums also integrate a tuning system. Six to ten tuning screws move a ring that presses against the skin, allowing the drummer to tighten or loosen the drumhead.

TUNABLE VS. NON-TUNABLE DRUMS ▶️

Tunable bodhráns have become very common for the modern player since they provide the player with increased control over the pitch, especially in various weather conditions. Hand tuners have become extremely common as well (versus using a key or screwdriver), allowing the player to tune quickly and efficiently. Tunable drums rarely have a crossbar in the back, but if they do, it is generally T-shaped, so the backhand is still able to move about. The drumheads tend to be smaller, and the shells are deeper.

Non-tunable bodhráns would be considered more traditional. They are more likely to have a crossbar in the back and painted décor on the front. Also, the drumheads tend to be larger in size, and the shells are shallow. The player can still tune a non-tunable bodhrán; it just takes a little extra work. Moisture can be used to loosen the head.

TUNING ▶️

As far as tuning, the drumhead should have some "give" to it. If it is too loose, the player will not achieve the proper response. If it is too tight, then the pitch will not change when moving the backhand, and it will have a high-pitched "ping" sound to it when struck. It will take some time to find the "sweet spot" when tuning. The drumhead is not tuned to a specific key, but rather a "feel." If the player owns a non-tunable drum and the head feels too tight, then squirting a small amount of water onto the backside of the drum and rubbing it in will help loosen the head.

NOTATION KEY

Conventional music notation is written as notes on a staff. A staff has five lines with four spaces—one space between each line:

Five-line Staff

Barlines

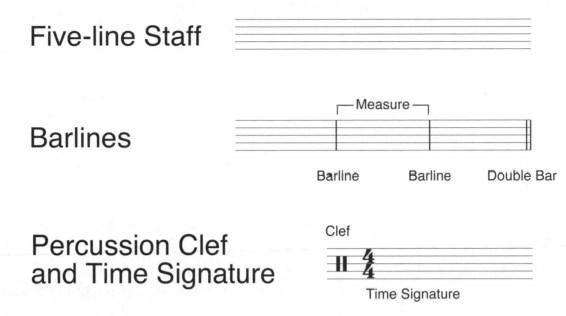

Percussion Clef and Time Signature

NOTATION SYMBOLS

The position of a note on the staff will determine the pitch of the note while also serving as a guide to where the backhand should be positioned when changing the pitch. There are different symbols for each backhand position on the bodhrán, which will make the notation easier to follow.

SLUR

A *slur* is a curved symbol that ties several notes together. In this book, it will be used to create a "run" from high pitches to low ones and vice versa on the bodhrán.

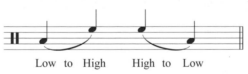

TIPPER DIRECTION

There will be various arrows and letters used to indicate the direction in which the player will move the tipper. (More on this later in the book.)

$\downarrow$ = Downstroke

$\uparrow$ = Upstroke

$\rightarrow$ = Tap

B = Back of Tipper

TR = Triplet

ACCENT

Accents are notes played with a greater emphasis. When a note has an accent symbol (>) or an arrow is bolded, then that note should be played louder.

$\uparrow\downarrow$ = Accent (any bold arrow)

READING NOTE VALUES

To be able to understand the lessons in this book, you will need to understand note values (how long each note lasts).

Each note symbol represents a different value. A whole note lasts for one whole bar (in 4/4 time), a half note's value is half of a whole note, and a quarter note's value is a fourth of a whole note. We can keep subdividing all the way down to what are called sixty-fourth notes. The note value tree shown below subdivides the note values down to sixteenth notes.

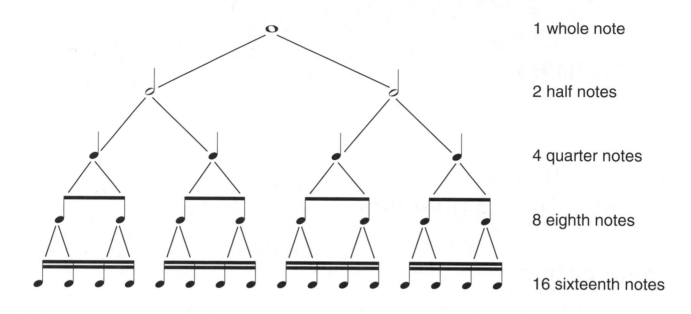

1 whole note

2 half notes

4 quarter notes

8 eighth notes

16 sixteenth notes

COUNTING

The majority of modern western music is notated and counted by dividing the rhythmic pulse into groups of four, meaning four separate beats. This is counted as: "1 2 3 4." These would be quarter notes.

You can then subdivide them into eighth notes: "1 and 2 and 3 and 4 and."

In this notation, we will use the "+" symbol in place of the word "and": "1 + 2 + 3 + 4 +."

Sixteenth notes: "1 e + a 2 e + a 3 e + a 4 e + a."

When playing many of the grooves in this book that are in 4/4, it is very helpful to count out all the sixteenth notes in your head. This will help you figure out where each hit lands.

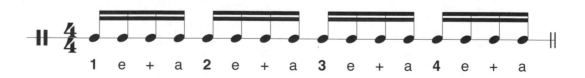

1 e + a 2 e + a 3 e + a 4 e + a

POSITIONING ▶

BODY AND DRUM

The drum is generally (and preferably) played in a seated position. Sitting up straight, the player should have a 90-degree angle formed between their torso and thighs. The drum will rest on the player's thigh. It should also be tucked slightly under the arm, touching the side of the ribs. Contact with the ribs helps to keep the drum sturdy when pressing or moving the backhand against the skin. However, if it is tucked back too far, then the drum will sound flat with no resonation.

The non-dominant hand should be free and placed at the top of the backside of the skin. Rest the fingertips on the backside of the drum. Making some contact with the fingertips helps to take away some of the overtones. Never place the hand completely flat on the skin, as this takes away all tone and makes the drum sound flat like a box.

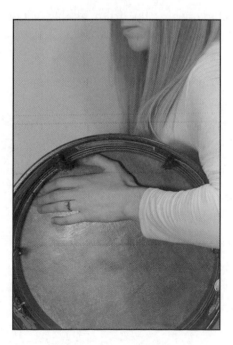 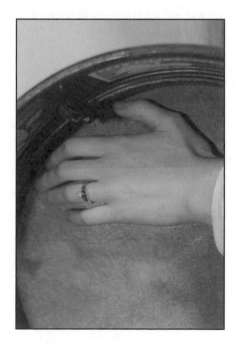

TIPPER AND WRIST ▶️

The drum is struck using the dominant hand and is played with a wooden stick, often called a *tipper* or *beater*. For those learning the Kerry-style sticking (which is where most begin), the tipper is held near the center. The player holds it like a pencil, between the thumb and index finger, with the second finger underneath the tipper for support. Then, rotate the tipper towards the torso. The end closer to the player is the portion that will be mainly used.

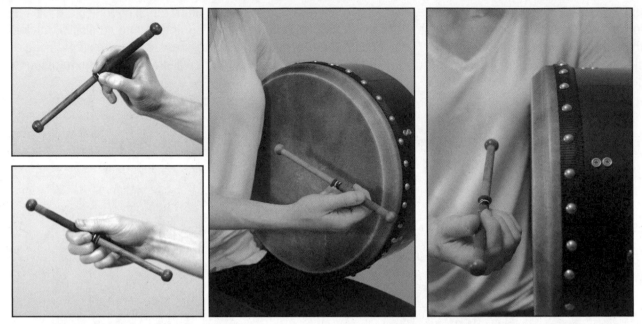

The movements should come from the player's wrist and not their elbow. The elbow can be tucked into the player's side. This will help the player focus on generating the movement primarily from the wrist.

The grip on the tipper should be firm, but it should not be a "death grip." A grip that is too loose will cause several bounces off the skin rather than one solid strike, and a grip that is too tight will cause the muscles in the hand to cramp.

The tipper should be almost parallel to the drum and very close in proximity to the head of the drum. Never angle the tipper more than 45-degrees away from the drumhead; anything more than that will put a strain on the wrist and cause the player to fall behind on their strokes. The closer the tipper is to the drumhead, then the tighter, faster, and more accurate the strokes can be.

The wrist and forearm should make a straight line; never bend the wrist in towards the drum, as this will put strain on the wrist and could eventually lead to injury.

There are several types of tippers. The traditional Kerry-style tipper has a knob on each end and is great for producing heavy, driving rhythms. Most beginners start with this style of tipper, but as one can see, the options are endless. Thin tippers can be used to produce specific notes and get more of a "pop" sound. The "click-stick" produces more of a jazzy, swing sound and feel (think of a brush on a snare).

It should be mentioned that there are various styles of using the tipper, one alternative notably being the "top end" style. For more on this, please see the Appendix at the end of the book.

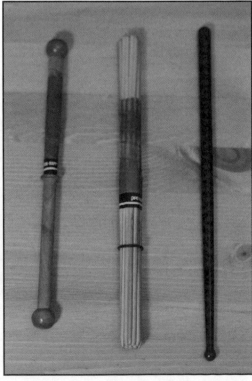

DOWNSTROKES AND UPSTROKES ▶️

The player should hear a solid strike every time the drum is struck. If one was to draw an invisible line, then it would look like a crescent moon shape regarding the motion of the tipper approaching the drum, striking the drum, and then coming off the drum. The wrist will make a motion similar to turning a doorknob.

Begin with the downstroke (naturally, the easier of the two). Start with the palm of the hand facing up toward the sky, and then slowly rotate the wrist towards the drum so that the inner side of the knob on the end of the tipper contacts the drumhead. Finally, continue the downstroke motion off the drumhead, with the palm facing the ground. Overall, there should be one solid motion with the wrist and forearm rotating. Work on perfecting a well-placed downstroke before moving on to the upstroke.

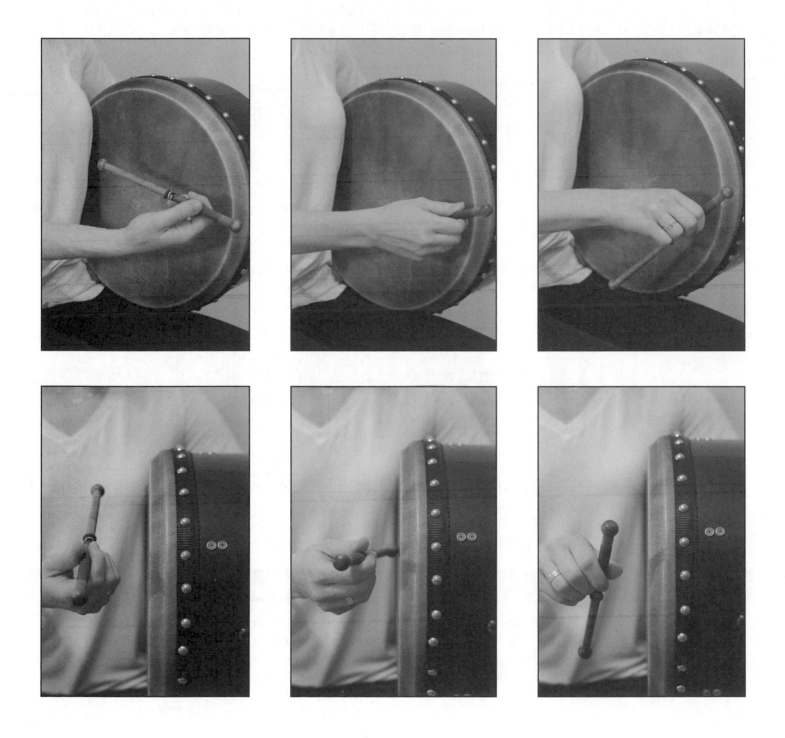

Downstrokes

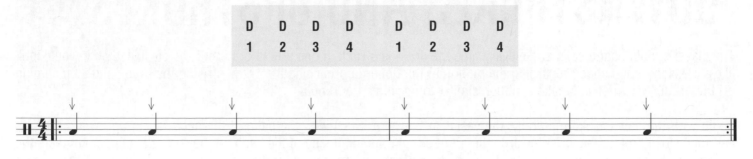

When ready, the upstroke should start with the palm of the hand facing down towards the ground. When striking up, slowly rotate the wrist towards the drum so that the inside side of the knob on the end of the tipper contacts the drumhead. And finally, continue the upstroke motion off the head of the drum, with the palm facing the sky. The player may need to take more time perfecting the upstroke. It's very common to hear more scratching or scraping as one works on developing the upstroke. The player may even miss the drum at times before achieving a solid upstroke technique.

Upstrokes

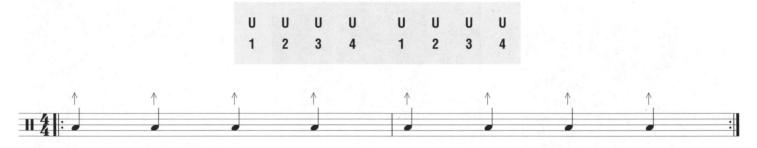

Once comfortable with each stroke separately, then put the two together. Always begin with a downstroke. When the player reaches this stage, it is recommended that they work with a metronome. This will allow technique and timing to develop together.

Downstrokes and Upstrokes

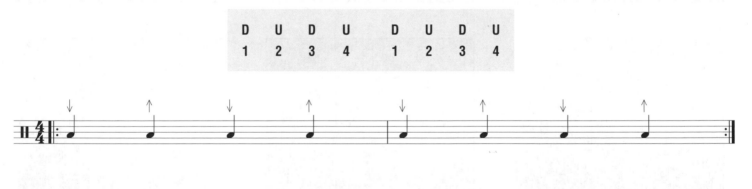

TECHNIQUE TIP

A few things to keep in mind while practicing: Make sure the drum is positioned upwards and straight. The player should not be too relaxed, therefore causing the tipper to miss the drum. Keep the tipper at a 45-degree angle and avoid opening it to a 90-degree angle, which can cause a scraping sound. Keep the arm planted and move only from the wrist. (If the entire arm starts to move from the elbow, then this could cause scraping as well.)

SPEED DRILL

This drill helps to develop the player's speed and accuracy using a metronome and shifting from quarter notes to eighth and sixteenth notes. The metronome not only helps with timing but can also give the player a chance to slowly work their way up by increasing the beats per minute (bpm). In looking at the notation, the player will see accented strokes (bold arrows), which should coincide with the click of the metronome. The last part of the exercise is what it would feel like to play a reel (4/4 time) up to speed. Start the exercise at 60 bpm, and over time, with a lot of practice and patience, slowly work up to 116 bpm (dance speed).

Quarter Notes

Eighth Notes

Sixteenth Notes

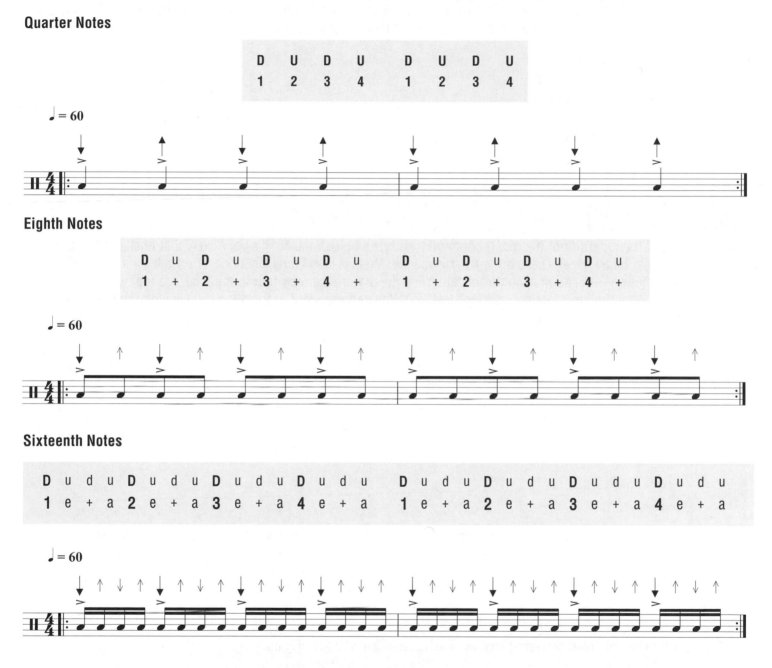

FEELING THE GROOVE

Players should train themselves to tap their foot to the beat while they are playing. The metronome can help guide the player in knowing when to tap. Every time a click on the metronome is heard, the player's foot should be tapping the ground. The earlier one begins implementing this exercise, the more quickly it becomes second nature. Many trad musicians tap their feet while playing. It especially comes in handy at sessions in pubs where the noise level can be particularly high, and sometimes, watching one another's feet is the only way to know if everyone is together. (For more about sessions, see the Appendix at the end of the book.)

TUNES

A large portion of trad was created for dancing. Tunes (*tunes* are purely instrumental; *songs* are sung with words) are generally divided up into two sections, an A part and a B part. Each part is eight bars. The dancers would take one part for the right foot and one part for the left foot. To play a tune in its entirety, one must play two A parts followed by two B parts. As always, there are exceptions to the rule (some tunes, for instance, have three or four parts while others are "single," in which only one A and B part are needed). However, the majority of tunes follow the AA BB structure. The repetition also makes it easier to learn the tune by ear, hence the success of the aural tradition. A set of tunes would typically consist of three tunes, and each tune tends to be played three times. A typical set looks like this:

- Tune 1: AA BB AA BB AA BB

- Tune 2: AA BB AA BB AA BB

- Tune 3: AA BB AA BB AA BB

REEL (4/4) ▶️

The *reel* is one of the most (if not the most) common tune types in Irish music. It's very likely that one would hear more reels than any other tune type at a session or a performance. A reel is in 4/4 time, counting "**1** e + a **2** e + a **3** e + a **4** e + a," with the accent (heavier stroke) on each downbeat. When the player taps their foot to the beat, the foot will tap on beats 1, 2, 3, and 4. It has a driving, "fast paced train" feel to it. You can use word association to help with the timing: **wa**-ter-mel-on. Always begin with a downstroke.

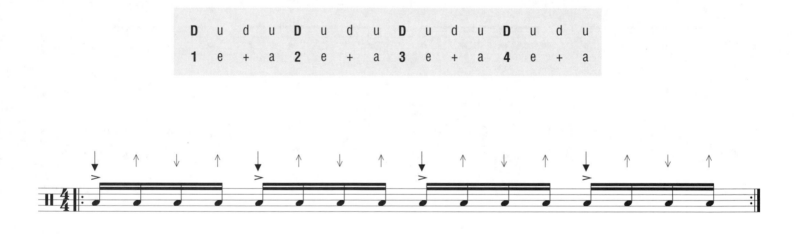

Here's a list of reels that could appear at any given session where you are playing:

- The Silver Spear
- Sligo Maid
- Castle Kelly

- Concertina Reel
- Merry Blacksmith
- Earl's Chair

On the next page is a reel mapped out in the typical two-part structure, with repeats incorporated within. You can practice this along with any of the tunes mentioned above.

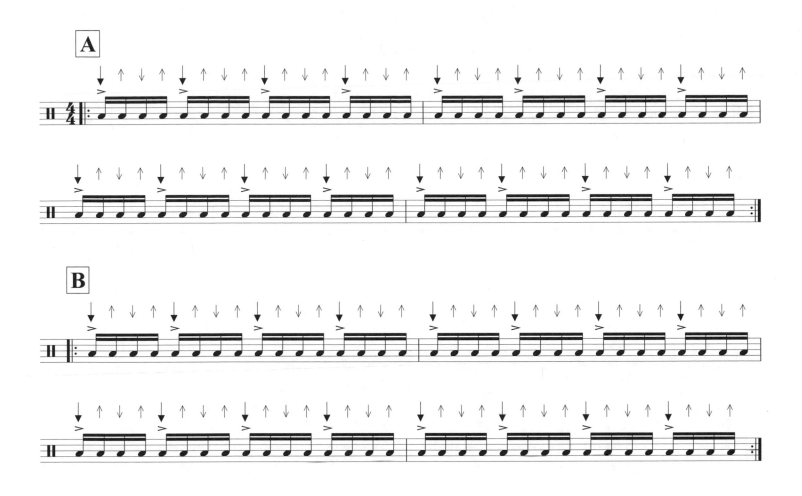

A

B

JIG (6/8) ▶

The *jig* is the second most common tune type in Irish music. Jigs and reels would be the two most well-known and heavily played of all the tune types. The jig is in 6/8 time, counting "1 2 3 4 5 6," with the accents on beats 1 and 4. When the player taps their foot to the beat, the foot taps on beats 1 and 4 while beats 2, 3, 5, and 6 are counted in between each tap. It has a "smooth ocean wave" feel to it because of the two accents present (as opposed to the reel with only one accent). A word association to help with timing: **jig**-i-tty-**jig**-i-tty. Again, always begin with a downstroke.

D	u	d	U	d	u	D	u	d	U	d	u	D	u	d	U	d	u	D	u	d	U	d	u
1	2	3	4	5	6	1	2	3	4	5	6	1	2	3	4	5	6	1	2	3	4	5	6

Here's a list of jigs you may encounter at any given session where you may play:

- Saddle the Pony
- Miss McCleod
- Kesh Jig

- Lilting Banshee
- Connachtman's Rambles
- Bill Collins' Jig

On the next page, a jig has been mapped out in the usual, two-part form. You can use it to play over any of the tunes mentioned above.

Practice, practice, practice! Before going any further in the book, make sure there's a solid foundation on both the reel and jig.

ADVANCED DRILLS

ACCENT DRILL ▶

The Accent Drill helps the player to work on accenting different notes throughout a pattern. The reel will be used as the base pattern for this exercise. In this exercise the player is challenged to venture off and try accenting the other three notes in the pattern. Take turns starting off with the basic pattern accenting beat 1, and then move on to the first upstroke, which would be the "e," then the "and," and finally the "a." This will benefit the player as they begin to progress and reach a stage where they are learning more tunes. They will realize that to follow the tune, it will require changing where the accents fall from time to time.

Accenting Downbeats

```
D u d u D u d u D u d u D u d u
1 e + a 2 e + a 3 e + a 4 e + a
```

𝅗𝅥 = 60

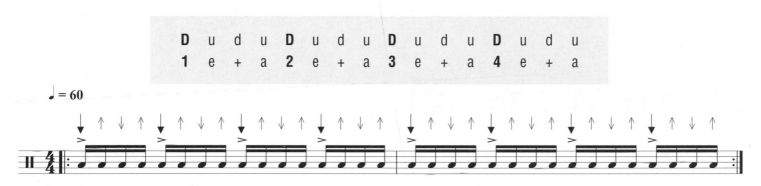

Accenting the "e" of Each Beat

```
d U d u d U d u d U d u d U d u
1 e + a 2 e + a 3 e + a 4 e + a
```

𝅗𝅥 = 60

Accenting the "+" of Each Beat

```
d u D u d u D u d u D u d u D u
1 e + a 2 e + a 3 e + a 4 e + a
```

𝅗𝅥 = 60

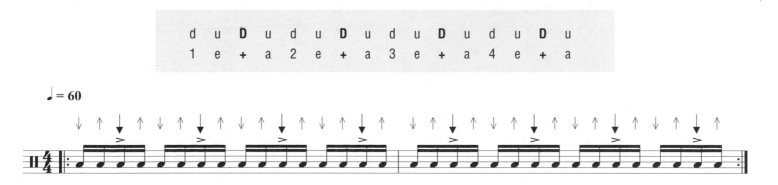

Accenting the "a" of Each Beat

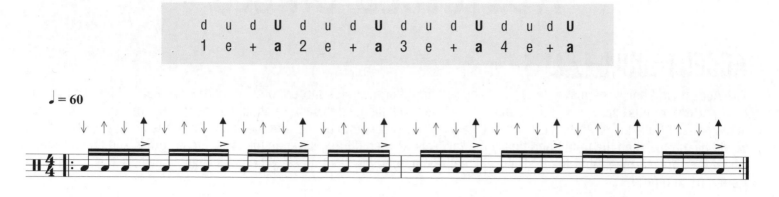

```
d u d U d u d U d u d U d u d U
1 e + a 2 e + a 3 e + a 4 e + a
```

♩ = 60

Going back to the speed drill that was taught earlier, this first variation takes the accent drill and implements it into the speed drill. Once the player reaches the sixteenth-note or third part of the speed drill, then they can shift to challenging themselves to accenting different strokes rather than just playing the basic reel pattern.

SPEED DRILL VARIATION 1 ▶

Quarter Notes

```
D U D U    D U D U
1 2 3 4    1 2 3 4
```

Eighth Notes

```
D u D u D u D u    D u D u D u D u
1 + 2 + 3 + 4 +    1 + 2 + 3 + 4 +
```

Sixteenth Notes

```
D u d u D u d u D u d u D u d u
1 e + a 2 e + a 3 e + a 4 e + a

d U d u d U d u d U d u d U d u
1 e + a 2 e + a 3 e + a 4 e + a

d u D u d u D u d u D u d u D u
1 e + a 2 e + a 3 e + a 4 e + a

d u d U d u d U d u d U d u d U
1 e + a 2 e + a 3 e + a 4 e + a
```

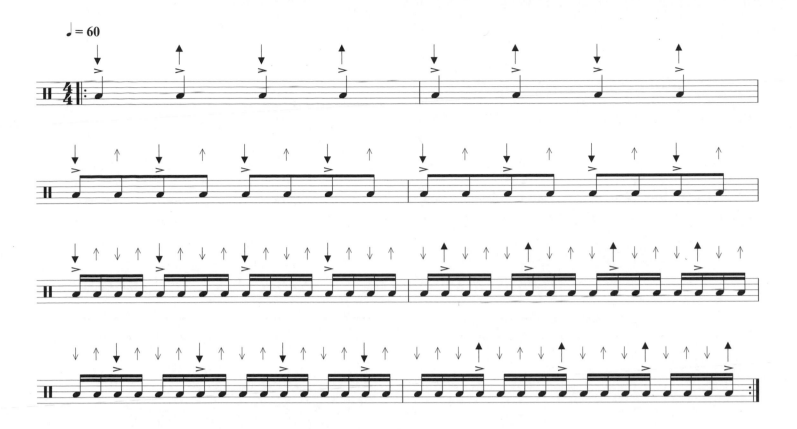

Finally, this second variation of the speed drill helps to continue to develop the player's speed, as well as challenging the player to think about shifting patterns without stopping. This will not only benefit the player in changing time signatures, but it will also help them recognize the difference in feel between the two patterns. The shift will happen at the sixteenth-note section or the third section of the speed drill, and the two patterns will be between a reel (4/4 time) and a jig (6/8 time).

SPEED DRILL VARIATION 2 ▶

Quarter Notes

D	U	D	U		D	U	D	U
1	2	3	4		1	2	3	4

Eighth Notes

D	u	D	u	D	u	D	u		D	u	D	u	D	u	D	u
1	+	2	+	3	+	4	+		1	+	2	+	3	+	4	+

Sixteenth Notes to Jig Pattern

D	u	d	u	D	u	d	u	D	u	d	u	D	u	d	u		D	u	d	U	d	u		D	u	d	U	d	u
1	e	+	a	2	e	+	a	3	e	+	a	4	e	+	a		1	2	3	4	5	6		1	2	3	4	5	6

ORNAMENTATION

IRISH TRIPLET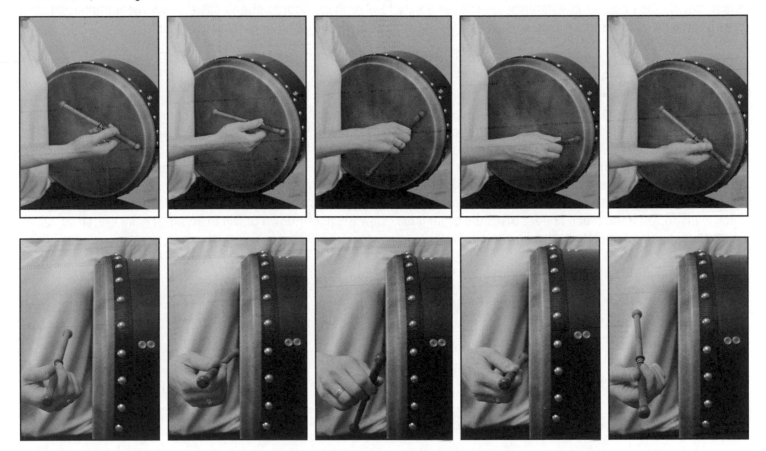

The name "Irish triplet" is used to denote an instance where three strikes of the tipper occur within one beat of the groove. Because of the more relaxed time feel that is used in Irish music, this "triplet" is more often notated as two sixteenth notes followed by one eighth note. The resulting rhythm blurs the line between a rigid, sixteenth-note rhythm and an equally spaced triplet within one beat. When producing a triplet, one should hear three strikes on the drum. The first and third strikes are the normal downstrokes and upstrokes, and the second is added in between (without disrupting the even amount of space between the first and third strokes).

The first note is struck as a downstroke with the end of the tipper closest to the torso. Then, the second hit occurs with a continuous downward motion (basically exaggerating the downward movement) until the back end of the tipper (the end further away from the torso) strikes the drum. Finally, follow through by coming back up, so that the third and final hit is an upstroke with the end of the tipper closest to the torso. The key component throughout this technique is to let your wrist do the work, making all three hits flow as one solid movement.

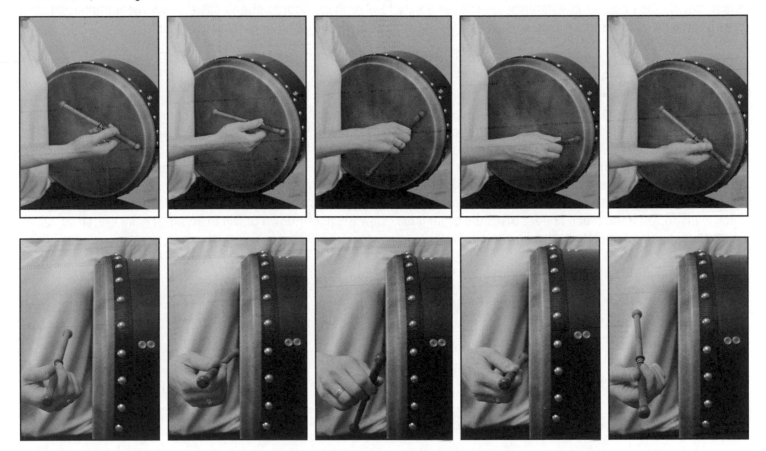

After developing the feel of the Irish triplet, try incorporating it into a basic reel rhythm. This will train your muscle memory to feel the difference between performing basic downstrokes and upstrokes versus extending the downstroke to catch the back end of the tipper when producing a triplet. (The triplet falls in place of the last two sixteenth notes.)

Irish Triplets in a Reel

D	u	d	u	D	u	d	u	D	u	d	u	D	u	d	u	D	u	dbu	D	u	dbu	D	u	dbu	D	u	dbu
1	e	+	a	2	e	+	a	3	e	+	a	4	e	+	a	1	e	TR	2	e	TR	3	e	TR	4	e	TR

Next, try incorporating Irish triplets into a basic jig pattern. (The triplet falls in place of beats 5 and 6.)

Irish Triplets in a Jig

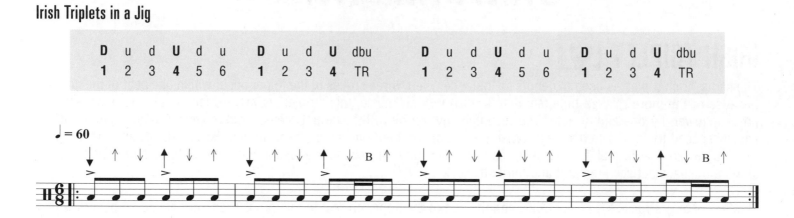

The goal is to be in control so that the player can deliberately place Irish triplets in any pattern when playing rather than random happenstance. Keep in mind that Irish triplets can be very difficult to play slowly. However, if the player can master them slowly, then control is established, with the ability to play these figures at any speed. It is recommended that a metronome be used for these exercises so that the player is assured they are not rushing the triplet.

RIMSHOT ▶

Similar to a rimshot on a snare (♩), the player can strike the edge of the bodhrán with the tipper and produce a "click" sound. Please note that the sound of a rimshot can be quite loud, and therefore, these should be used very sparingly. The player can produce them on either an upstroke or a downstroke. The upstroke tends to be easier, coming up and catching the edge of the bodhrán (near the bottom of the drum) on the way up. For a downstroke, it's easiest to roll the drum away from the player's ribs and catch the side of the drum that's closest to the body (rather than trying to come down on the top of the drum). It takes practice to finesse the strike. The player needs enough of the tipper to catch the edge so that a click is heard, yet if too much tipper strikes the drum it may slow the player down or trip them up. Try the exercises below, incorporating a rimshot into both a jig and a reel.

Rimshots in a Jig

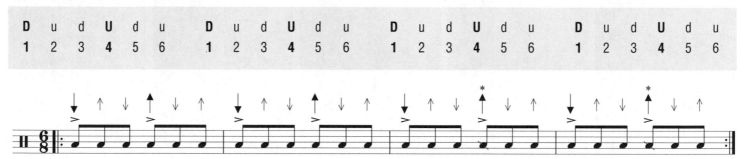

Rimshots in a Reel

VARIATIONS

A *variation* is taking the original pattern and making some type of change to it. This can include incorporating alternate sticking, using the backhand to manipulate the pitch, switching where the accent falls, eliminating strokes, or varying the volume. Here are a few exercises that will help the player develop some simple variations.

ALTERNATE STICKING: DOUBLE DOWNS ▶

Another version of sticking is called *double downs*. Instead of strictly playing down, up, down, up, down up in succession, this alternate sticking throws a second down in the mix. The second downstroke is referred to as a "tap" since it's truly not a full downstroke. The pattern morphs into "down, up, tap, down, up, tap." To tap into the drum, the player must start by having their palm face the sky and then rotate inward to the drum, leaving the palm facing the instrument. Then, rewind the movement with the palm facing the sky once again.

The tap stroke is more of a hit into the drum. As always, it is up to the wrist to do all the work. Neither the fingertips nor the forearm should be moving in and out. Only the wrist rotation is what causes the tipper to strike the drum. After mastering the tap movement, the player can move on to incorporating it in succession with a downstroke and upstroke.

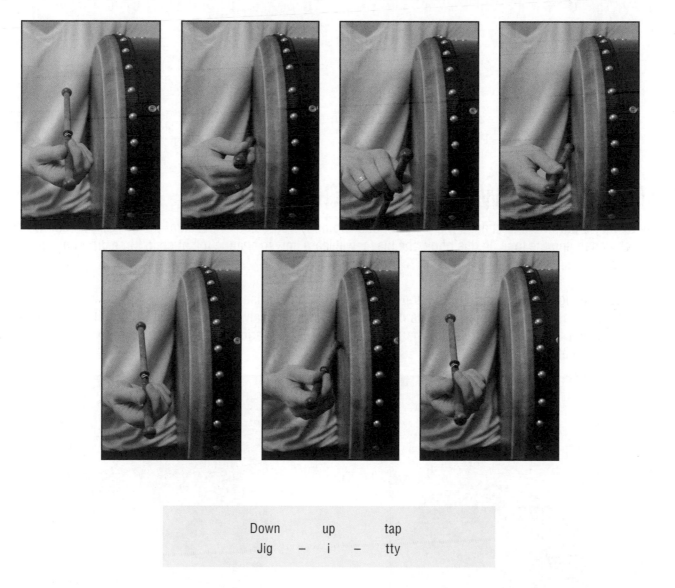

23

Next, the player should practice the double-down sticking within a jig pattern. It fits more naturally into the jig, since the jig is a three-feel, necessitating a movement of three strikes.

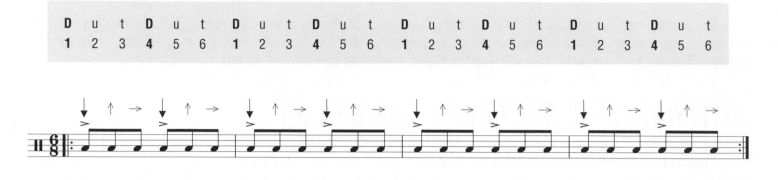

Finally, the player should practice implementing both sticking styles within the same pattern. For example, in a jig, try two bars of normal sticking and then two bars of double downs, alternating between the sticking styles. The goal is to become comfortable when moving between the two approaches.

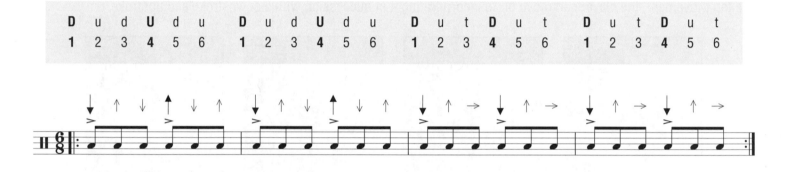

CHANGING PITCH WITH THE BACKHAND ▶️

One way to vary a pattern is to change the pitch. In pushing on the backside of the skin, the overall pitch of the drum will raise, thereby changing the tone. In this book, the player will learn how to change the pitch in three different ways, all using the backhand.

The first is by pushing in with the heel of the non-tipper hand. This will raise the overall pitch, giving it a warm, round tone. Never directly strike the heel with the tipper, as it will deaden the sound; always play out in front of it. The triangle symbol is used to represent the use of the heel on the notation. Practice the various exercises on the next page to get used to incorporating the heel.

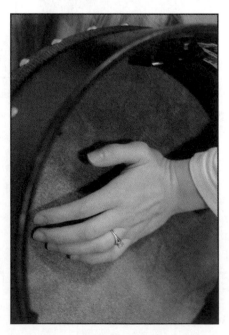

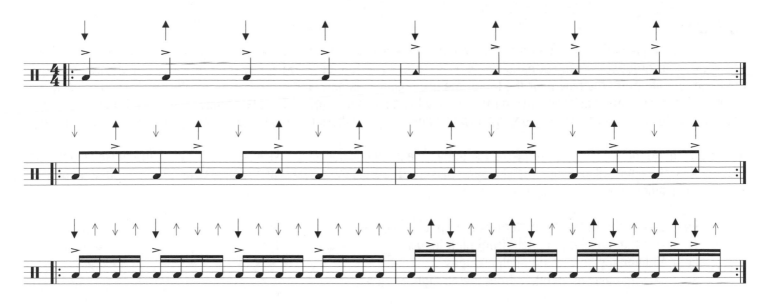

▶ 6:44

The second way to change the pitch is by pushing in with the long edge of the thumb and thick part of the palm. This will create a "pop" or "snap" sound in addition to a crisp tone. For downstrokes, the tipper should strike just above the thumb; for upstrokes, the tipper should strike just below the thumb. The "X" symbol is used to represent the use of the thumb within the notation. Practice the various exercises below to get used to incorporating the thumb.

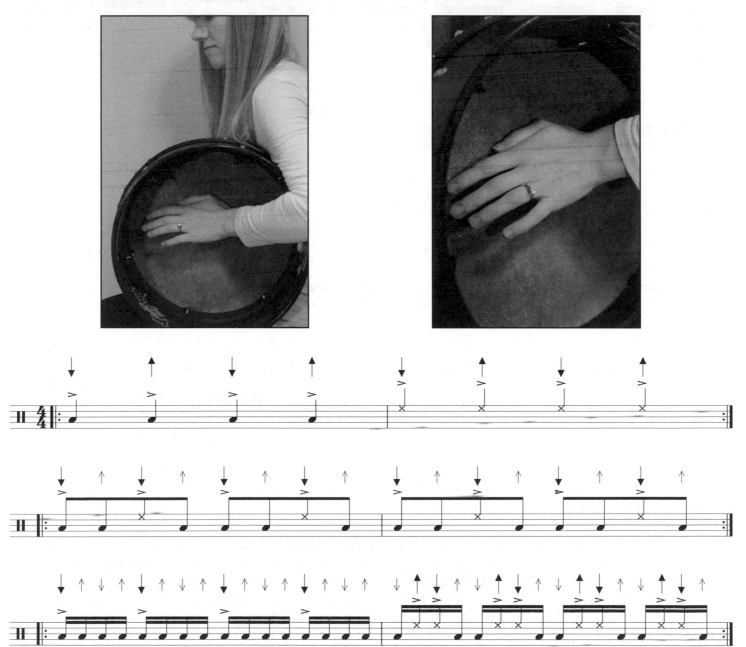

The third technique is to push in with the thumb and thick part of the palm, slowly moving vertically along the backside of the drum to produce a "run" of either highs to lows or lows to highs. To explore the full spectrum of pitch changes, the tipper should primarily play near the top of the drumhead. It is natural to want to move both the tipper and backhand together. The player must concentrate on moving only the backhand. (Note—The player may need to shift their movement of the tipper to "in and out" versus "up and down," depending on where the tipper is vertically placed on the drumhead.)

As the backhand moves away (down) from the tipper, the pitch will descend. Likewise, as the backhand moves closer (up) to the tipper, the pitch will ascend. The slur symbol is used to alert the player that a run is taking place within the notation. Practice by playing these exercises in sequence:

1. Four sets of the basic reel pattern with no pitch changes
2. Four sets that descend in pitch, from high to low
3. Four additional sets with no pitch changes
4. Four sets that ascend in pitch, from low to high

Changing Pitch from High to Low

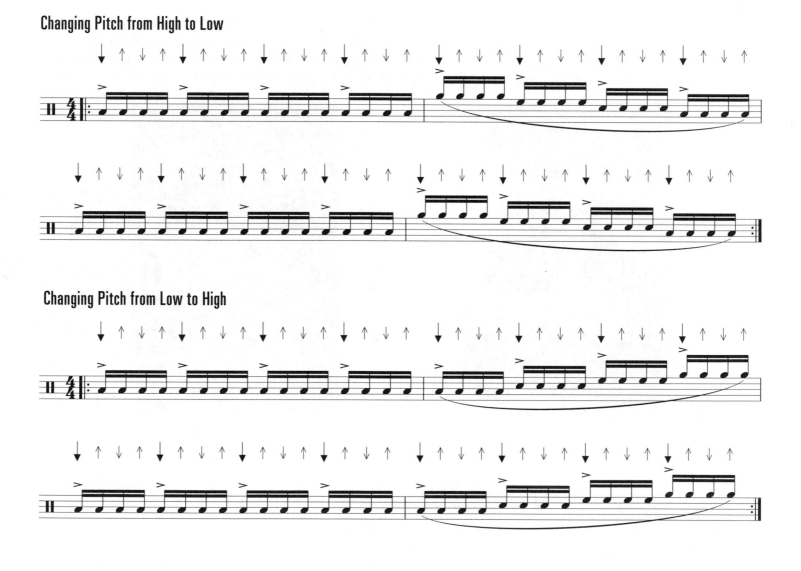

Changing Pitch from Low to High

BACKBEAT ▶

One of the most common variations for the reel is accenting the *backbeat.* This exercise will incorporate both changing where the accent falls and the use of the backhand. The player will change the accent from the basic pattern (on beat 1) to the backbeat (on the "and" of beat 1). To make the accent stand out even more, incorporate the backhand by pressing the thumb and thick part of your palm into the back of the drumhead and have the tipper strike it just above the thumb. The player should visualize the points between the thumb and the top of the drum to be their new playing space. This will create a "pop" sound.

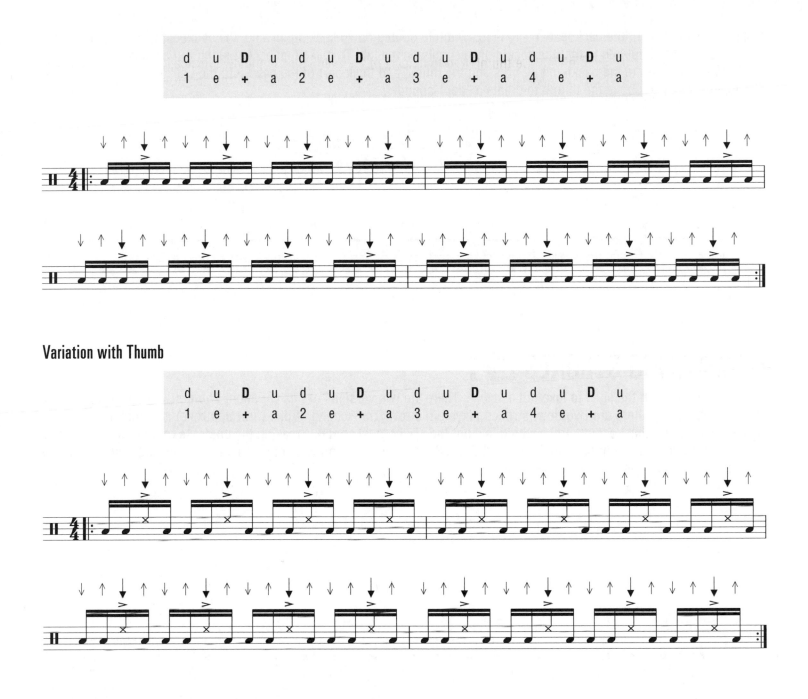

Variation with Thumb

Next, the player should work on incorporating the backbeat into the basic reel pattern to feel more comfortable moving in and out of the variation. Start with four counts of the basic reel, and then move into four counts on the backbeat, alternating back and forth between the primary feel and the backbeat variation.

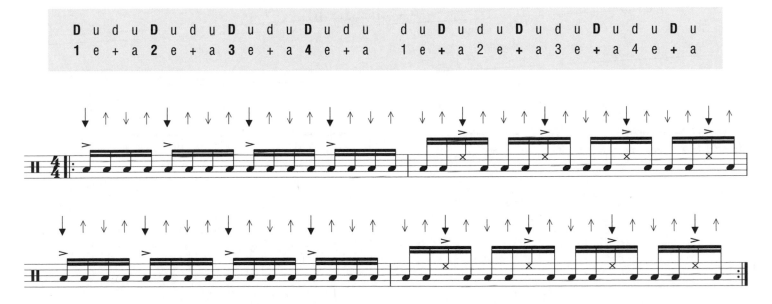

A simple way to accent the backbeat in a jig is to switch to double-down sticking. In a jig, the backbeat falls on beats 3 and 6. Double downs simplify it in that the accent always falls on the tap. To make that accent stand out even more on the tap movement, incorporate the backhand by pressing the thumb and thick part of the palm into the back of the skin and have the tipper strike just above the thumb to create a "pop" sound.

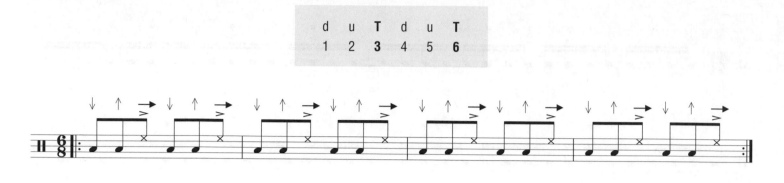

ELIMINATING STROKES

A simple variation on the jig is to take out a stroke. There are two versions of this variation. The first will be referenced as "two-downs" since there are two downstrokes played in a row. The second stroke (first upstroke) is eliminated. Here, a space exists where that second stroke would fall, but the player must continue making the upstroke motion to arrive at the next downstroke. The counting would be "1 (2) 3 4 5 6," and the tipper movements would be "down (up) down up down up." In this variation, beats 1 and 3 are accented.

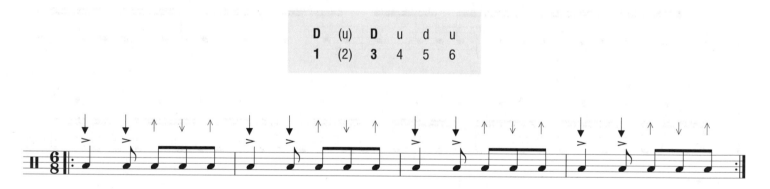

The second will be referenced as "two-ups," since there are two upstrokes played in a row. The fifth stroke (third downstroke) is eliminated. In this case, the counting would be "1 2 3 4 (5) 6," and the tipper movements would be "down up down up (down) up." In this variation, beats 4 and 6 are accented.

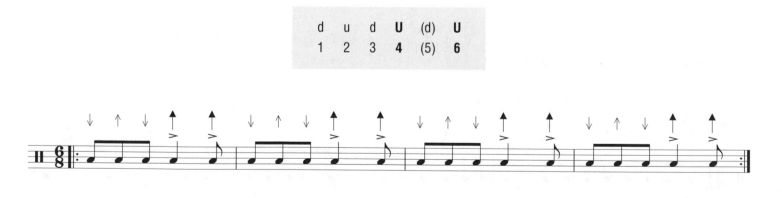

To keep the proper spacing and timing in between the movements, utilize the motion of the downstroke or upstroke that has been eliminated; just pull away from the drum as not to strike it.

Once comfortable with both variations on their own, the player should then incorporate each variation into a sequence with the basic jig pattern. Again, this will establish a comfort level for the player in being able to move in and out of variations.

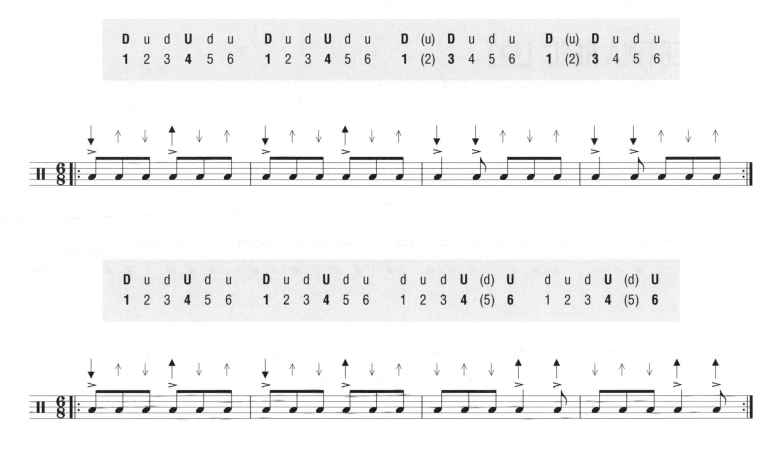

DYNAMICS

A simple, yet often overlooked way to create variety is the use of *dynamics* (volume). First, the player should always be sensitive about their volume. The bodhrán should never dominate; rather, it should neatly fit into the mix. A common way to implement variations in dynamics is to build from playing soft to loud. This can be especially useful at the end of a tune when preparing to repeat it or when going into a new tune altogether.

DISSECTION OF TUNES

Now that the player has mastered several variations, stickings, and ornamentations, it's time to put everything to use. The following section shows two complex notations of a reel and a jig. In mapping them out, the goal is for the player to understand how to train their ear to listen for where these variations may fall. Eventually, the player should be able to incorporate these variations to allow themselves to internalize the tune more effectively. Remember, the following examples are simply a starting point. The main point to keep in mind is that it is eventually all about improvised interpretation, so the player may hear something different than what is mapped out below.

"CONCERTINA REEL" ▶

During the first time through this tune, play just the basic reel pattern. The player should always be aware of the driving rhythm. Once that is established, play through the form a second time and attack only the A part and its complex notations. After the A part is mastered, then move on to the B part. Finally, play the tune in its entirety. The player can start by following the written music, but the goal should be to eventually play the tune without the aid of the notation.

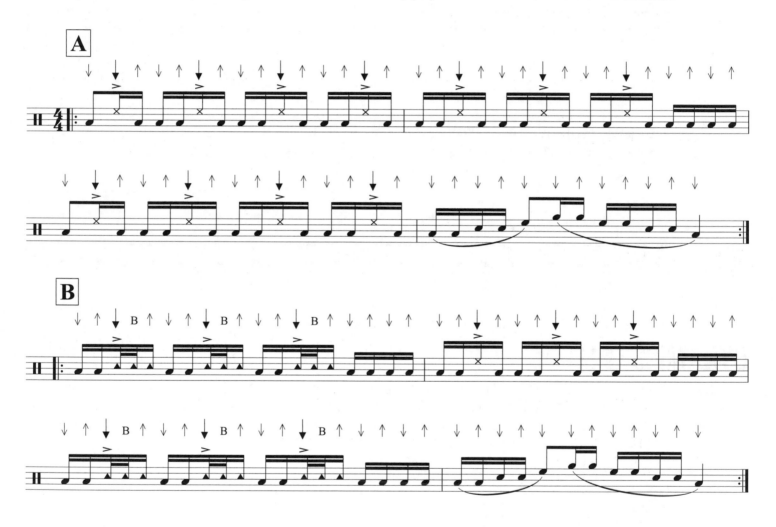

"SADDLE THE PONY" ▶

Play the basic jig pattern during the first time through this tune. The player should always have the flowing rhythm of the jig permeate the foundation of their playing. Once that is established, go through the form a second time and attack only the A part and its complex notations. After the A part is mastered, then move on to the B part. Finally, play the tune in its entirety. The player can start by following the written music, but the goal should be to eventually play the tune without the aid of the notation.

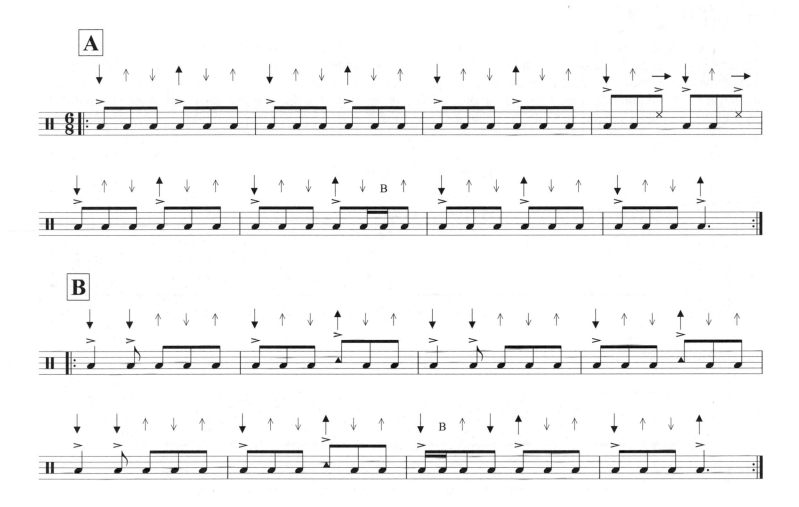

ADVANCED TUNE TYPES

The reel and jig are the two most important tune types to master. However, once the player is well underway with those forms, it is fun to dive into some of the other tune types that may come up in a session. Below are a few patterns to get the player familiar with some of these other tune types.

HORNPIPE

This is a tune type in 4/4 time, counting "1 + 2 + 3 + 4 +," with accents on each downbeat. The main difference between the reel and the hornpipe is that there is a heavier "swing" feel to the hornpipe, which means that there is a slight pause after each downbeat. The backbeat (beats 2 and 4) is also slightly accented, which differentiates it from a typical reel. To make the backbeat stand out even more, incorporate the backhand by pressing the thumb and thicker part of your palm into the back of the drumhead and strike it with the tipper just above the thumb to create a "pop" sound.

Here's a list of hornpipes you may encounter at a session:

- Boys of Bluehill
- Rights of Man
- Cronin's Hornpipe
- Stack of Barley
- Plains of Boyle
- Off to California

SLIP JIG

The *slip jig* is a tune type that is traditionally danced only by women, often in soft shoe. It is important to keep this in mind while also being aware of the volume and intensity when playing. The slip jig is in 9/8 time, counting "1 2 3 4 5 6 7 8 9," with the primary accent on beat 1 and other accents falling on beats 4 and 7. These three accents are where the player should tap their foot. Since it is in 9/8 and that is an odd number, notice the accent stroke (first stroke) changes direction. The first set of nine pulses starts on a downstroke, and the second set of nine pulses starts on an upstroke. To break it up a bit, use the heel of the hand to lift the accent on the second set of nine pulses.

TECHNIQUE TIP

If the player switches to down-up-taps or double downs, then the accent will always fall on a downstroke. Some players like applying that sticking since downstrokes tend to be easier to accent than upstrokes.

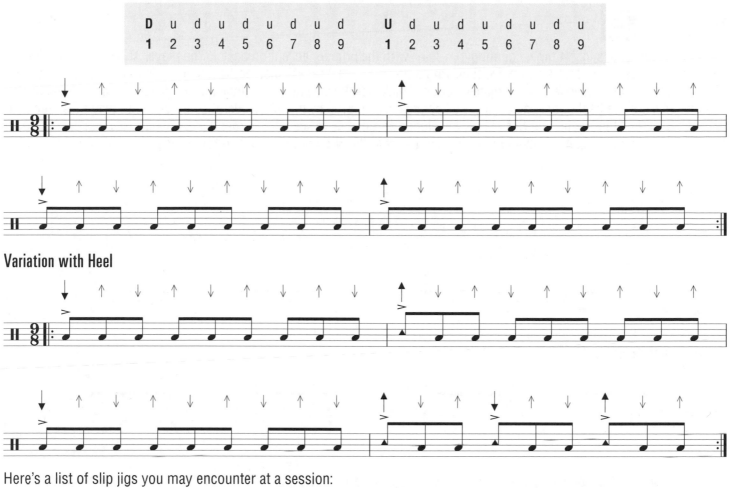

Variation with Heel

Here's a list of slip jigs you may encounter at a session:
- Butterfly
- Drops of Brandy
- Kid on the Mountain
- The Rocky Road to Dublin
- Barney Brannigan's
- Fig for a Kiss

SLIDE ▶

The *slide* tune type is often thought of as a fast-paced jig. However, the accenting on a slide can vary greatly from a jig. It tends to pack its punch more on the backbeat. It's often characterized as having a "choppy ocean wave" feel to it rather than the smoothness of a jig. Slides are a tune type commonly used in *set dancing* (a form of social dancing like square dancing), and in watching the dancers foot movements, the instrumentalists developed the basic pattern below. The slide is in 12/8 time, with the beats grouped in four sets of three pulses, occurring on beats 1, 4, 7, and 10. However, the accents fall on beats 1, 4, 6, 9, and 10. To add more flavor to the rhythm, incorporate a small amount of the backhand. Push the thumb and thick part of the palm in for beats 4, 5, and 6, and push in the heel of the hand to round out beats 9 and 10.

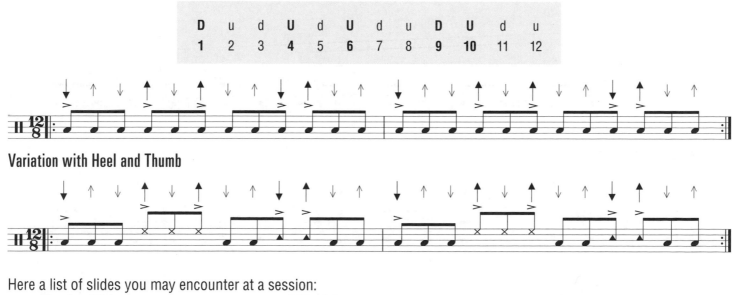

Variation with Heel and Thumb

Here a list of slides you may encounter at a session:
- Brosna Slide
- Star Above the Garter
- O'Keefe's
- Dingle Regatta
- Dennis Murphy's
- Merrily Kiss the Quaker

POLKA

The *polka* tune type is in 2/4 time, counting "1 + 2 +," with the primary accent on beat 1. The player should tap their foot to this primary accent. Try to stay away from playing a polka as a "fast reel." Instead, focus on really popping that backbeat (the "ands") to lift the groove. Try to create a "boom-chick" feel by accenting the upbeats with a pop (push with the thumb and thick part of the heel of the backhand). Polkas are easily played by melody players, so they tend to play these tunes at a rapid pace. The "tap" technique was simply developed as a means to keep up! Rather than playing really fast up and down movements, the player can simply tap into the drum so that the wrist doesn't have to rotate or do quite as much work.

Another option for the polka is to play with an alternative time feel, with different parts of the beat accented throughout the groove. This is a way to still play upstrokes and downstrokes but without feeling as rushed. In this version, the foot will tap on all the downstrokes, which fall on beats 1 and 2. However, notice that the accents fall on beat 1 and the "+" of beat 2 in the first measure, with a final accent on beat 2 of the next measure. To add more flavor to the rhythm, try to incorporate a small amount of backhand technique. Push in the heel of the hand to round out "+" of beat 2 in the first measure, and then push in the thumb and thicker part of the palm to pop out beat 2 in the second measure.

POLKA (ALTERNATIVE TIME FEEL)

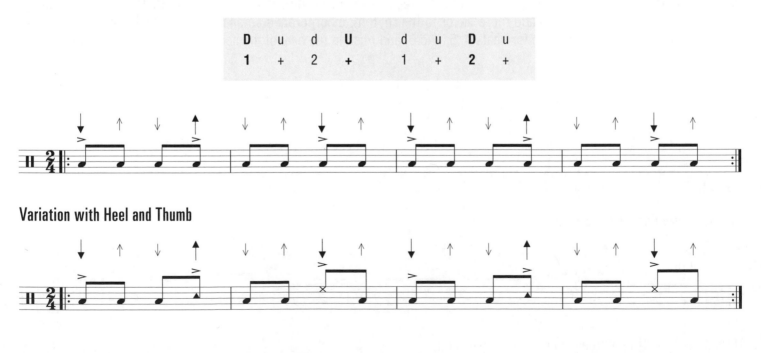

Here's a list of polkas you may encounter at a session:

- Kerry Polka
- Ballydesmond No. 1
- Britches Full of Stitches
- Ballydesmond No. 2
- Little Diamond Polka
- Terry Teehan's

OTHER RHYTHMS AND GROOVES

Below are a few fun rhythms and grooves to test out on the bodhrán. Note—These rhythms should be used sparingly and carefully when playing with others. Ultimately, the tune creates the rhythm, so these grooves should not be forced upon a tune that already has a proper feel to it.

MOTOR RHYTHM (JUNIOR DAVEY)

This is a fun take on the backbeat while also incorporating an Irish triplet. It's a very common, go-to pattern in reels that has been popularized by Junior Davey.

D	(u)	D	u	d	u	D	D	u	d	u	D	u	d	u	dbu
1	(e)	+	a	2	e	+	a	3	e	+	a	4	e	TR	

MODERN GROOVE ("JAMES BROWN MARCH" BY MICHAEL MCGOLDRICK)

This is a fun take on a classic James Brown groove, first popularized by Michael McGoldrick.

D	u	d	u	D	u	d	u	d	u	D	u	d	u	D	u		d	u	D	u	D	u	d	u	D	U	d	u	D	U	d	u
1	e	+	a	2	e	+	a	3	e	+	a	4	e	+	a		1	e	+	a	2	e	+	a	3	e	+	a	4	e	+	a

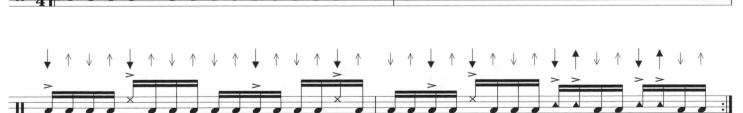

35

ODD METER (TUNES IN 5 OR 7) ▶

It is rare in trad music to see tunes in odd or asymmetrical time signatures, but tunes that are written in either 5/8 time or 7/8 time can be a good challenge for the player to wrap their head around. The main challenge is figuring out how to handle even-grouped pulses with odd-grouped pulses within the same measure. The pulses grouped in twos are easy enough, but the pulses grouped in threes can be tricky. If the player thinks of the first pulse as a downstroke, the second pulse as an upstroke, and the third pulse as a tap, then it's easy to swap around the sets of numbers to create different variations within the counting.

5/8 Time

7/8 Time

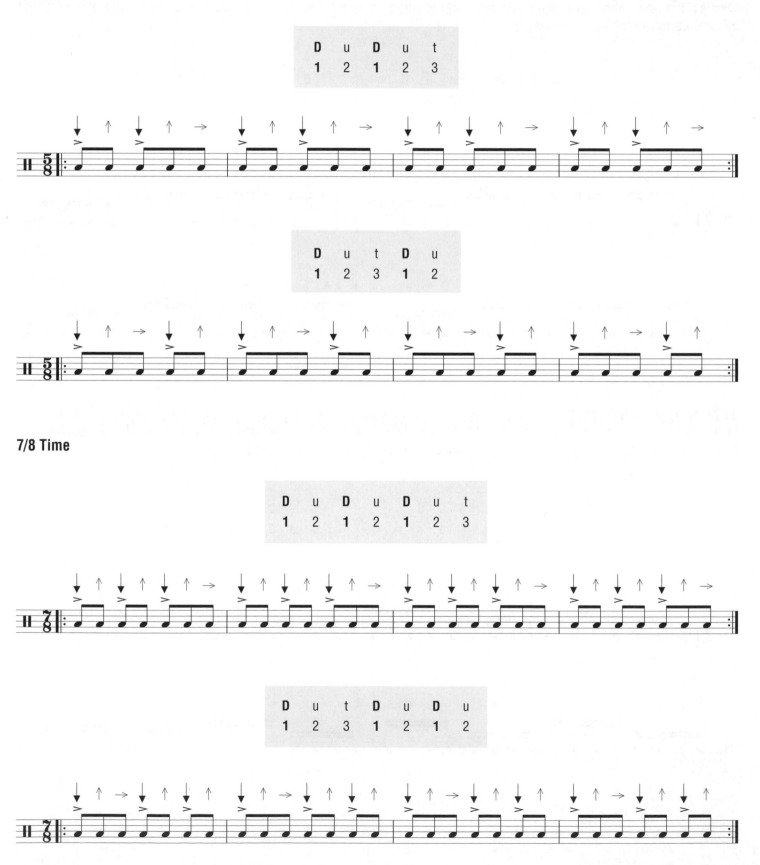

APPENDIX

The Role of the Bodhrán

Known as "the heartbeat of trad," the role of the bodhrán is to ultimately keep the beat. However, unlike rock or other music styles, the bodhrán player should accent and highlight the rhythm, not create it. The rhythm itself comes from the tune and how it is played by the melody player(s). The bodhrán should match the beat and follow the music. In order to follow the music, the player must learn the tunes and songs that make up the repertoire.

Ideally, the player should know the tune well enough that they can hum it. Keep in mind that even though one may be familiar with a specific tune, each melody player will more than likely put their own spin on it. Therefore, keeping one's ears and eyes open is always crucial for a bodhrán player's awareness. The bodhrán can also be thought of as the "glue" that keeps everyone playing together.

Sticking Styles (Kerry vs. Top End)

The traditional style of playing and the one most commonly taught to beginners is Kerry style. Kerry-style sticking comes from County Kerry in the southwestern region of Ireland. This style uses two ends of the tipper, which typically has a ball or knob on either end, and it is held more towards the middle. The strokes are made using up and down motions, while most of the playing happens near the middle of the drum, where more driving rhythms are produced.

A modern style that has developed over the last 20 years or so is the *top end* style. Players generally use a thin tipper that is held at the top end so that only the bottom end of the tipper strikes the drum. The stroke movements travel in and out, and most of the playing occurs at the top end of the drum, where the notes tend to "pop" more. The player tends to follow the accents of the melody as well.

There is no rule that a player has to strictly play one style over the other. In fact, it is highly encouraged that the player creates their own unique style by pulling bits and pieces from each approach and fusing the two together.

Session Etiquette

A *session* is an informal gathering of musicians where music is played. Since the bodhrán is one of the cheaper trad instruments that looks easy to play, it is taken up by many people. However, it is not always learned properly or taken seriously, thus producing "players" that may disrupt a session rather than add to it. So as not to add to that stereotype, here are a few unspoken rules and guidelines that are important to know and consider before participating in a session:

1. **Always ask to sit in at the session.**
   Generally, there is a leader who kicks off most of the tunes. He or she is the best person to ask.

2. **Take turns.**
   If there is more than one bodhrán player at a session, the players should take turns. Since there can be a lot of improvised interpretations when it comes to bodhrán playing, It's very easy for things to get messy if more than one person is playing the bodhrán.

   In following the rule of one drummer at a time, it is then customary to take turns after every set (a set is generally three tunes). The leader will typically give a vocal "hup" or lift a foot to let everyone know the set is ending.

3. **Know the tune.**
   If the player does not know the tune, or more importantly, the tune type, then they should not play. Most tunes are repeated several times, so if the player feels familiar enough with the tune after the first or second time, then they can jump in.

4. **Always be aware of volume.**
    If in doubt, start quietly and work your way in. It can also help to listen to the guitar or any other rhythm section instruments that are being played.

5. **Ultimately, remember that the tune is everything.**
    The bodhrán player should support the tune, not take away from it. This is because Irish music is primarily a social type of music. Rather than closing one's eyes, it's much more useful for the player to always be aware by looking around and keeping their head up. A lot can be said with something as simple as making eye contact or with the lift of a foot.

6. **Finally (and most importantly): don't forget to HAVE FUN!**

RESOURCES

Makers

With the popularity of the bodhrán on the rise over the last few decades, many bodhrán makers have surfaced (with more on the horizon). Below are a few suggestions. However, the list is not meant to be exhausted. Having a bodhrán built can be a very personal experience, so it is important for the player to do their research in finding out which maker is best for them. If the player is simply looking for a basic, "beginner" drum, then they may want to check their local music store. If the player is looking to have more input in how their drum looks and feels, then they may want to reach out to a maker. Body shape and taste in sound vary greatly from person to person, so having a bodhrán built to the exact specifications of what is the best personal fit can be worth the extra time and money.

Mike Quinlan–mqdrums@gmail.com

Seamus O'Kane–*www.tradcentre.com/seamus*

Rob Forkner–*www.metloef.com*

Walton's–*www.waltonsirishmusic.com/bodhrans*

Michael Vignoles–*www.michaelvignoles.com*

Gordon Falconer (Falconwood Tippers)–*www.falconwood.nl*

Note—Amy currently plays drums built by Mike Quinlan. The one used in the tutorial videos is a Quinlan.

Recommended Artists and Recordings

Below is a list of bodhrán players and their associated band(s) and recordings that are worth checking out. The list covers a wide variety of styles, so be sure to listen to their albums in addition to searching for video clips on YouTube. It is truly indispensable how much one can learn not only from listening, but from watching others play as well.

Kevin Conneff and Peadar Mercier (The Chieftains)

Junior Davey–*A Sound Skin*

Donnchadh Gough (Danú)

Tommy Hayes and Mel Mercier (Stockton's Wing)

Cathy Jordan (Dervish)

John Joe Kelly (Flook)

Dom Keogh (Mórga)

Johnny McDonagh and Colm Murphy (De Dannan)

Jackie Moran (Comas)

Brian Morrissey (Buille)

Eamon Murray (Beoga)

Ronan O'Snodaigh (Kíla)

Colm Phelan (Goitse)

Amy Richter (áthas)

Frank Torpey (Nomos)

Robbie Walsh (Perfect Friction)

Aids for Practicing

The *Comhaltas Foinn Seisiún* Volumes 1, 2, and 3 are great albums to use as a starting point for learning tunes. Each track is a single, traditional tune played several times. These tunes will assuredly appear in any given session, so the player should become familiar with them.

Any version of an app that slows audio down is essential for learning and practicing. These apps allow the player to pull in any tune off their playlist and slow it down to a speed that grants more achievable results. After slowing the tune down, the player should slowly work their way back up to full speed with precision and accuracy. There are many free apps available.

Any version of a metronome app is also essential. Many of the drills in this book become twice as useful if played along with a metronome. There are many free versions available.

Attend a *céilí* or *set dance* (forms of Irish social dancing.) These tunes were originally created for dancing, so learning tunes is greatly enhanced by watching a dance and seeing how the music and movements work together. As a drummer, the footwork can especially help the player develop patterns that they may not necessarily think of by listening only to the melody.

HAL LEONARD DRUM & PERCUSSION METHODS

HAL LEONARD CAJON METHOD
by Paul Jennings

This beginner's guide for anyone learning to play the cajon takes you through the basics of the instrument and its techniques with dozens of exercises and over 30 grooves from many genres including rock, Latin, blues, jazz, flamenco, funk, and more. There are also more advanced techniques in the final chapter that include how to change the pitch with your foot, playing with brushes, and playing rolls with your fingers.

00138215 Book/Online Video $12.99

HAL LEONARD DJEMBE METHOD
by Paul Jennings

This beginner's guide takes you through the basics of the instrument and its techniques. The accompanying online videos include demonstrations of many examples in the book. Topics covered include: notation • bass and slap tone exercises • three- and four-tone exercises • basic rhythms • traditional djembe rhythms • modern techniques • and much more.

00145559 Book/Online Video $12.99

HAL LEONARD DRUMSET METHOD
by Kennan Wylie with Gregg Bissonette

Lessons in Book 1 include: drum setup & fundamentals • tuning & maintenance • basic music reading • grips & strokes • coordination & basic techniques • basic beats for many styles of music • 8th notes, 16th notes, dotted notes & triplets • drum fills • and more. Lessons in Book 2 include: limb independence • half-time grooves • syncopation • funk grooves • ghost notes • jazz drumming • chart reading • drum soloing • brush playing • and much more.

00209864 Book 1/Online Media......................$16.99
00209865 Book 2/Online Media......................$16.99
00209866 Books 1 & 2/
Online Media, Comb-Bound...........$27.50

HAL LEONARD DRUMS FOR KIDS

Drums for Kids is a fun, easy course that teaches children to play drumset faster than ever before. Popular songs will keep kids motivated, while the simple, easy-to-read page layouts ensure their attention remains focused on one concept at a time. The method can be used in combination with a drum teacher or parent.

00113420 Book/Online Audio..........................$12.99

HAL LEONARD HANDPAN METHOD
by Mark D'Ambrosio & Jenny Robinson

The *Hal Leonard Handpan Method* is written for a broad range of skill levels. Beginners will find the introductory material and exercises necessary to develop their touch and technical skill, while the advanced player will find instructions on how to execute high-level techniques, create sophisticated sounds, and build complex patterns. The information, techniques, and theory presented in this book are designed to be flexible, and can be adapted to work on your instrument, no matter the scale or number of notes. The price of this book includes access to videos online, for download or streaming, using the unique code included with each purchase.

00288061 Book/Online Video $14.99

HAL LEONARD SNARE DRUM METHOD
by Rick Mattingly

Geared toward beginning band and orchestra students, this modern, musical approach to learning snare drum includes play-along audio files that feature full concert band recordings of band arrangements and classic marches with complete drum parts that allow the beginning drummer to apply the book's lessons in a realistic way.

06620059 Book/Online Audio..........................$10.99

HAL LEONARD STEELPAN METHOD
by Liam Teague

The *Hal Leonard Steelpan Method* is designed for anyone just learning to play the steelpan. This easy-to-use beginner's guide takes you through the basics of the instrument and its technique. It covers: stance • holding the mallets • types of strokes • tone production and volume control • stickings • rolls • scales • calypsos • many songs and exercises • basic music reading • steelpan anatomy and maintenance • steelpan history • and more.

00111629 Book/Online Audio..........................$12.99

See these and many other percussion titles at
halleonard.com

Order today from your favorite music retailer at **halleonard.com**
Prices, contents and availability subject to change without notice.